MW01092816

The Pictures

The Pictures

MAX WINTER

Tarpaulin Sky Press
Saxtons River, Vermont
2007

The Pictures
© 2007 Max Winter

First edition, February 2007.
ISBN-10: 0-9779019-2-0
ISBN-13: 978-0-9779019-2-0
Printed and bound in the USA.
Library of Congress Control Number: 2006931674

Cover design by Max Winter.
Book design by Christian Peet.
Text is in Adobe Caslon Pro. Titles are in Georgia Tall.

Tarpaulin Sky Press
Saxtons River, Vermont
www.tarpaulinsky.com

The Pictures is also available in a limited hand-bound edition
from Tarpaulin Sky Press.

For more information on Tarpaulin Sky Press perfect-bound
and hand-bound editions, as well as information regarding
distribution, personal orders, and catalogue requests, please visit
our website at www.tarpaulinsky.com.

Reproduction of selections from this book, for non-commercial
personal or educational purposes, is permitted and encouraged,
provided the Author and Publisher are acknowledged in the
reproduction. Reproduction for sale, rent, or other use involving
financial transaction is prohibited except by permission of the
Author and Publisher.

Contents

Still

Moving

Still

4 by 4

A black
and relatively round
stone.
It looks smooth,
at least at this distance.
Dirty blond sand
beneath it, combed
into squiggly rows.
It is possible that the rows have meaning.
It is possible that the stone has meaning.
The stone is near the upper right corner,
as if to suggest the shape of its enclosure.
There is a faint gleam
at one point of the overcurve,
oh white sun.
At the left edge,
the snout of a scorpion.
Hard to believe, but
it must be true.
We almost don't want to look.
Although nothing will happen next.
And some places there are
where scorpions are quite common
in all seasons.

4 by 7

In the desert, a car sits by itself.
It is a dark brown, with white splashes of dust.
One long horizontal flame floats
from its bumper to its front door.
Heat waves rise off its hood.
A mountain rises behind its trunk.
A century plant, un-bloomed, to its left.
A blue gym bag, with one stripe,
far to our right.
It is opened,
and it is not evident there is anything inside the bag.
There is a dark spot beside the bag,
not large enough to be significant,
but noticeable, as if liquid had been poured for no
    reason.
And here, in the middle of the desert.
The car door to our right is open, too.
An empty plastic bag rests beneath the accelerator.

5 by 4

A perfectly centered portrait,
it stands out.
Short cropped blond hair,
could have been cut off an interstate.
Blue eyes. Fair skin.
Looks smooth, fairly unblemished.
A grim face, but then you notice
it's simply the way the mouth is constructed.
The lower lip that protrudes slightly.
The upper lip designed by a committee,
divided twice by two faint scars,
trickling into the lip's flesh,
more like furrows when you are
too close. Nostrils that flare
then rein themselves in.
A small, compact nose,
pores clogged,
red in spots.
The eyes are deep, the lashes long,
a little tired today, maybe?
Though slight, he wears a t-shirt
that suggests physical fitness
though that may not be the case.
It could be the squaring of the shoulders
or the upright semi-strident posture.

You'd have to say *scared*
or *overly humble,* though,
when presented with the complete picture,
when scanning the face.
You would have to wonder
what has been there.

5 by 5

The day bright, and gone.
The door rises from the grass.
It may not be a door
but simply an opening.
The walls around the opening are thick, gray, stone.
There is a crack to the right of the gaping dark.
At the base, looking freshly arrived,
six yellow flowers,
curving in different directions.
Behind the doorway a track
no longer used,
ties overgrown with weeds.
At the upper left, a plane,
leaving a white trail pointing downwards
or upwards, depending on the perspective
of the person in the cockpit.
The grass around the blackness is green,
looks damp,
shines occasionally.
The faintest haze of a chain link fence, in the distance,
a small parking lot beyond it, possibly
one yellow dusty truck parked,
or possibly just waiting,
an eruption of water from a hydrant,
the sense that if we want to know where

we are, we are not,
even if that has been said before.
A black beetle, crawling around the door
to the center
of the world,
a slip of leaf in its pincers.

5 by 7

The man's feet are not in the picture.
His arms point towards the ground beneath us
limply, as if broken.
His hands are also absent.
The ends of his thick mustache point upwards.
The ends of his mouth,
like his arms,
point towards our feet.
His lips: thick,
and stretched by what must be a smile.
He wears a white unitard,
smudged near what must be the navel,
knees, cock, balls, nipples evident.
It is impossible to say
what suspends him.
There is no background,
only white.
What sheer years
spent just
like this.
Bless him
once before you leave,
twice in case I forget.

6 by 4

Five individuals, grouped
in an off-white yard.
The one-story house behind them
is white, with a black roof.
A little bit of smoke stopped
as it leaves a brief chimney.
They stand in height order,
smallest to tallest,
left to right.
The smallest one is so small
he is barely standing.
He wears a box-shaped hat
nearly covering his dark eyes.
He has small lips,
possibly mashed together.
He is not smiling.
Beside him a small girl,
dark stringy hair to her shoulders.
Black dress,
buttons down her middle.
Feet in shiny shoes,
pointed straight ahead.
One hand on hip,
one on the little one's shoulder.
She is not smiling.

Beside her, a man,
hair slicked back,
eyes upon us,
arms folded,
white shirt,
white pants,
white shoes,
black suspenders.
Moon-shaped head.
He is not smiling.
Beside him,
a woman with her head askance,
squinting,
wearing an off-black checkered dress,
a white shirt,
holding one bunch of black roses.
She is not smiling.
Set apart,
farthest right,
an older man,
possibly chubby,
striped shirt,
black suspenders,
hands at sides,
head up,
slight growth of beard.
He is not smiling.

His eyes.
We cannot see
what he is doing
with his eyes.

7 by 4

Between the bridge and the branch, roughly
ninety-seven stones.
Some round,
some rectangular,
some neither, just
small.
Water flowing around them,
towards our feet.
On half of the stones,
well nigh over fifty,
thick green moss.
Six leaves at irregular intervals,
extending back into the trees
fallen upstream.
Thirty-seven tadpoles.
One dead minnow, floating
near the lower left corner.
A bird with great black wings,
about to land
or about to dive,
who among us
would say which is which,
between us and the water.
Beside the river,
a bucket

with a little thick-legged sprite
dancing on its side.
A white naked body,
female,
wavy blond hair,
back turned to us,
bending down
over a pyramid of stones,
standing in the water
she cannot feel.

7 by 8

A man is standing naked,
his back turned.
He is tall and medium weight,
his skin often pink-tinged and hairless.
A woman is lying in bed,
also naked,
facing him.
Some of her long dark hair
spreads out over her chest.
Her breasts
flattened but not small,
the red of her areolas only slightly darker
than the pink of his skin.
One of the woman's legs is arched,
the other flat.
Her eyes are squinted, slightly.
There is a lamp on the bedside table
and a light in the fan, both on
and yet the room still seems dim.
There may be a radio on in the corner.
There is no painting on the wall but one
small painting of a house beside a river.
We cannot tell if air is moving through the room.
Or if it is needed.

7 by 10

The stage is made of dirty,
well-aligned boards.
A woman stands in the center,
in black, both arms crooked,
hands pressed just off center
of her chest. There is a man at the bottom
of the stage, one hand on his hip,
one hand raised in the air.
He and the woman both wear dark clothes,
darker than even Black and White can tell us.
Another man stands on the ground to our right,
arms folded, arms full of folders.
Every sound
only predicts
the silence that follows it.

7 by 12

Asphalt roof
behind yellow brick wall
rimmed by red clay fluted brick.
Puddle in which we see
mostly clouds, some sky,
today a blanched blue.
Beyond the puddle another partition,
this one flecked with white,
topped with red,
once again,
one big chip in a partition.
Across the dirty gray-black valley,
another roof, more manicured,
this one step-shaped.
Upper step: two small palms, one fern,
one woman, blue shorts, bent over.
Lower step: one man, one chair,
one red sweatshirt, one white table,
two magazines, one glass, one thirst.
The picture says
the rest is not important
or it would lie in the foreground.
What I see here
if I may make a leap
is the newly written
covering
the erased.

7 by 16

There is light
coming from outside the frame.
Several lights, converging
to make a circle on the hull.
The ship is long and black
on the bottom, white on the top,
curved in a valiant curl
at its prow.
The water is black.
A man is hanging
or so it seems
from the edge of the boat.
His legs are at a wild angle.
It is clear he wants to run
but there is no ground beneath him.
He is looking towards his hands
which extend above him.
Or if he is not looking at his hands,
he is looking for a face
which only he
and possibly some others
might recognize.
Other things are here, too:
lights across the water from this dock,
a yellow rope

surfacing in three spots before it goes out of view,
and bills, lots of them,
floating on the water.
We cannot see their denominations
but, given everything,
they're probably pretty large.
Sirens seem a likelihood, too,
if not helicopters.
The mist is important,
although there is no mystery
by this point.

7 by 24

The wall is white and stippled unevenly.

There are faint patches of dirt running along its rim.

On our left is a man in a white shirt, white pants and a chef's hat.

He holds a ladle slack in one hand.

His eyes are closed.

He is looking into the air, as if trying to remember something.

He has a mustache in its earliest stages, just a little bunchgrass beneath his nose.

To the right of him stands another man in the same clothes, though he has a white spot on his left cheek, no mustache.

He is very thin, has very red lips.

He is looking to the left of us.

His hands are in his pockets.

He is wearing white gloves.

He is sweating under his armpits. You can see the circles, you expect them.

To the right of him stands another man wearing the same costume, but perhaps less well, if we can judge.

One side of the shirt is untucked and hangs over a hip.

The other is tucked too tightly and looks taut against his side.

His cheeks are pale, and his eyebrows are sharp.

He has wilted.

Beside him is a quite, quite dirty man.

He wears a white shirt, white hat, black pants.

In each hand an empty voluminous pot.

The stains on his shirt are red (2), black (3), and green (3).

He looks prepared for what may come.

Beside the men, to our right, sits a Mercedes.

The interior is dark, but we see a man's nose and lips.

The nose is fleshy, the lips thin.

The chefs have not been paying attention.

And no one has been watching them.

This is the way we agree to behave.

If we live in Los Angeles, off Wilshire Boulevard, in 1998.

8 by 8

The man and the woman
sit in metal-backed lawn chairs
in the yard of their house.
The house is of yellow-gray brick.
The back of the man's head
rests against the back rail
of the lawn chair.
His mouth is open,
his eyes are closed.
The woman holds a magazine open
in an L-shape,
the perpendicular page curved
so that it hangs
over the page she is reading.
There are three large clouds in the sky,
one so large it stretches
from one horizon to another.
Half a plastic gorilla
raises its arms beneath a tree.
The man's pale legs sag,
in varying degrees,
to the viewer's left.

8 by 9

As if on both sides of a hallway,
two men stand, looking away from us.
One man has clearly dropped a shopping bag at
    his feet.
The street between them is empty.
A young man with dark hair runs away.
We have caught him in mid-stride,
one arm raised.
In his hand is a gun.
The gun looks bigger than the hand.
In certain ways, it could be said
to be larger than the boy's head.

8 by 10

In the white kitchen,
white with square-tiled walls,
white with swirls of smudge
baked in,
most people are looking down.
On our left,
a medium-height man,
40-ish,
silvery black hair,
pressed tuxedo,
mouth hanging open,
one hand extended beside him
as if waiting for a tool.
To the right, a meek boy, dark hair,
thin mustache, lips pursed,
white uniform,
looking at the tuxedo,
or perhaps at the man,
we don't know.
Beside them, the largest man
in the room, tilted to one side,
looking down as well,
face bright red,
a serious look
on a face probably rarely serious.

Looking down
under a raised panel
into darkness from which extends
a hand
holding a lobster
blurred because living.
The rest of us might blur as well
were we in such a position.

8 ½ by 11

A long street,
its lines slanting
towards the invisible.
The light yellowed,
though the picture's date is recent.
A bus stands beside a sign, door open.
A woman in a short-flowered skirt
and a black translucent blouse
looks away from us,
but not at the bus.
But at what?
We cannot say for sure
due to the angle at which her back is turned to us.
At this moment,
a young man in dark corduroys
steps into the vehicle,
a slight smirk on his face,
hair drooping to his neck.
The smirk, like the hair,
may have been there before.
He looks down, as if not thinking.
Who could blame him.
In five minutes it will rain.
Thought will be no more necessary
and no less essential.

9 by 9

Her face is probably familiar to a lot of people, but not by much. It's one of those faces in which no one feature is remarkable. Medium-sized nose, not unusually large lips, ears flat, eyebrows thin. If there's anything about her that might be called unusual, it's her make-up. It's been said that a person's sanity is in inverse proportion to the intensity of their make-up. And this woman's make-up . . . The lips are not just pink, they're a deep pink that looks freshly painted, could leave tracks on the air. The eyes are shaded dark blue, the whites stand out. And currently the whites point upwards. You know, or should know, looking at her, that she is not trying to remember something, not having a vision, that there's some larger role being played out. She's probably in one of the helping professions. But that's just conjecture. The mouth, in its current pose, is certainly that of one who is concerned. The lips are pursed, as if she were shaming something, or someone, or as if some great misfortune had just occurred. Which it could have. She's standing in a dark public space; you can see blurred bodies around her. She's leaning up against a red post, and you can see that, on the other side of the post, there's a sign. What the sign says is fairly predictable: "Wet Paint." We see it backwards, through the paper, as it is thin—and also some of it is bent, so you can get a hint of the message. And yet she leans against the post, unworried that the paint might stain her black jacket, made of some sequined material, thin, see-through, you see the pink shirt, also somewhat diaphanous, beneath it. If you're the sort of person who craves physical interaction with the artworks, you might want to reach forward and straighten her up. She seems to have hunched into her frown, in a way that suggests she's used to the frown, not much used to other facial expressions, though, which they say is bad for you, in the papers, if you have time to read the "health" column. And she does not, really and truly, look healthy. Her hair is poking out at five different angles, could be the wind. But there is no wind underground. No use in worrying, here, about what the hair is all about, or what the person is all about, because that never really comes forward in a purely two-dimensional medium. And the train, the subway train, whose tracks are evident beside her, a dim canyon, a place where we expect rats and empty cups, shoes and empty boxes, the occasional charred leaf, the occasional fallen bird, the occasional blind spot, the occasional sun mote, the train never comes.

10 by 10

One red stone.
One green stone.
One grey stone.
One white stone.
One black stone.
One black stone.
One blue rock.
One red stone.
One white stone.
One orange stone.
One half needle.
One green stone.
One white stone.
One tan stone.
One peach pebble.

One muddy stone.
One shining stone.
One lost stone.
One corner of a tool.
One pink shred.
One red stone.
One cut stone.
One magic stone.
One smooth stone.
One earth-shaped stone.
One plain stone.
One forgotten stone.
One water drop.
One epic stone.
One holy stone.

One turquoise stone, reflecting.
One plastic ess.
One wet tan stone.
One blue stone.
One glass stone.
One hollow stone.
One arrowhead.
One brown stone.
One brick stone.
One yellow stone.
One half stone.
One pine cone petal.
One green stone.
One eye stone.
One blue stone.

One black stone.
One white stone.
One wide stone.
One story stone.
One evil stone.
One blessing stone.
One recently piled stone.
One useless stone.
One blind stone.
One inching stone.
One aptly put stone.
One brown stone.
One
Stone
You

10 by 12

Two women under an un-pictured light.
One dark tan, the other white.
Reaching their arms up
and together under the light,
one reaching left, one reaching right,
joining at the top.
Probably the completion of a dance
step soon to be begun again.
They do not hold themselves as
those behind them do,
some reaching forward, some back,
some smiling, some neither smiling
nor frowning, just absorbed.
The others in the room
do not look like them:
shapeless grey pants,
angular Hawaiian shirts,
forgettable white tube tops.
These two women are self-possessed,
the way they are dressed
an indication of an indication.
The brown suede jacket on the one,
the white sweater on the other,
the black leather skirt on the one,
the pink dress on the other,

the upturned face and fastened shut eyes of the one,
the down-cast face, the open eyes of the other,
the shiny black shoes,
the open-toed faintly blocky sandals,
the knit stockings,
the bare smooth legs,
the full black lips,
the thin white mouth,
glossy black shoulder-length,
blond, stringy, pretty, nice,
the curled fingers
locked with upright fingers.
Even the incline of a foot:
one right foot off the ground,
one left foot touching by a toe.
It is possible they will not return
home tonight, or that there is no home
but in these simple remembered gestures
committed in a room with others,
all listening, all swallowed up.

11 by 11

The woman's mouth is open,
possibly as wide as it can go.
She is thin, and older than 50.
Her eyes are pinched,
and her arms are stretching towards us,
her hands in fists.
Her skin is dark.
Her skin is rough
and her face indicates
that the emotion we see
has been her only emotion,
with occasional deviations,
for several weeks.
Her hair has been braided once
and falls over her left shoulder.
She wears a black shirt
whose sleeves are rolled
but hang loosely around her elbows.
Her white pants are quite dirty.
It is hard to tell what is behind her
with all the dust,
but we think we see buildings and cars.
Something is moving around her.

19 by 19

The weather is dull today
though there is no evidence of that.
Not much presented
from where I sit.
Black, white, something else.
A grid, all lines pointing
towards a tiny center.
The space between lines
grows greater
towards the edges
as if a finger
pressed down
on the city's heart,
if there is such an organ.
If you get too close you can see
swimming pools, parking lots,
colonnades, lampposts, side streets,
thoroughfares, industries,
cars leaving, cars entering, cars making illegal turns,
and the occasional person,
or rather the occasional head,
in motion, like everything else.
The parks' locations are clear:
patches of grey
interrupted by squibs of pond-from-above.

Buildings of the same shape
travel in packs
towards or away from the center,
houses of the same shape
spill outwards,
possibly ingratiating themselves
to people on their way somewhere else.
This is all fascinating but
cannot explain the inexplicable
areas of dark near the center,
areas that must be quite large
in my crude conception of scale.
They are dark with white flecks
poking up, like grains
on blank parchment—
in reverse.
All somewhat circular,
edged by incomplete shapes:
a square with three corners,
an oval with a point,
a rectangle after a brush
with a celestial hatchet.
Two of these spots, to my count,
though the more you look, you will see
the picture is full of such areas, only
of different sizes and one thinks
different degrees of significance.

Though extrapolation like this
is painful because needless,
it is probably safe to say,
given the empirical evidence,
that the city is not at its best,
that best is in the distance,
vanishing as you approach it.

Moving

3 Minutes (The Ant)

The ant is standing
approximately two inches away
from a pastry crumb
dropped at 10:32 this morning.
The ant lifts its head up briefly,
swivels it around, and then
heads to its left, towards a pebble
equidistant with the crumb.
The ant crawls on top of the pebble,
then crawls over it,
then walks around it one and a half times,
then walks past it, towards a clump
of grass, isolated in this new yard.
Three blades, rising at different tilts towards light,
but all young.
The ant spends some time in the grass,
a long time, for an ant.
Two minutes, three seconds.
It then begins to emerge from between the blades,
head still, antennae moving slightly.
It is looking directly, we think, at the pastry crumb.
Interestingly, by the time the ant remembers
its original destination,
that destination point has shifted inexorably.
The air is heavy and dark.
A drop begins to fall towards the earth.

4 Minutes

The room where we sit
is cold.
The shapes on the screen
are indistinct.
One prone human
grows another human
from his chest.
The new-grown human
keeps reaching downwards,
and then we realize
these are not grasps but punches,
and that is a wide-brimmed hat on his head.
The remainder of the cowboy
makes no movement.
We begin to move backwards,
until we find ourselves behind
a dirty-blond, somewhat tousled head.
The head makes two very slight movements:
two looks to the right,
one long,
then one short,
almost immediately afterwards.
We know the punches continue
because the sprouted cowboy's head
appears, at regular intervals,

to the right of the neck beneath the head
that now fills the screen.
The intervals grow more dispersed.
The camera now rises,
and we could rise with it.
The punches stop.
You hear the sound of a body standing up,
barely a rustle.
Though we only see the head and shoulders,
the tensing evident in the neck
suggests movement in the arms,
very slight, very slight.
For twenty or twenty-five seconds,
the screen is completely silent.
Then, an explosion,
then another.
No more motion.
We move backwards again,
and our view reveals
a man standing by a table,
head down,
hand slowly resting a gun
beside a glass of whiskey
one quarter full.

5 Minutes

We are eye level with
a red, concrete wall.
Sand rises above the wall
and goes back down below the wall
in small tan staggers.
A yellow scoop rests, sort of,
on the sand.
The scoop, a set of squarish jaws, closed.
A pair of plastic rods
extends upwards from the scoop,
connected at a ninety-five degree angle
to another pair of rods,
reaching out of the frame.
The upper rods move back and forth.
Three times gently.
Four times with more force.
Twice roughly.
The plastic jaws open,
touch the sand, stay open,
then trip shut, a faint snap.
There is a splash of sand quickly following.
The jaws lift.
They swing back, around, away from us.
For a moment there is only the mound of sand.
Then a tire scrape.
A shoe tip

at the right side of the screen.
You hadn't noticed
and yet it was there,
significant.
It moves.
Now two shoe tips.
You hear the sound of things being moved.
You hear words you do not understand.
The apparatus lands in full view
in the middle of the frame.
A deep incomprehensible voice speaks firmly.
A smaller voice answers.
The wind across the microphone.
Nothing.
Nothing.
Seven or eight sniffs,
each three to five seconds apart.
Nothing.
A little hand with sand on its back
rights the apparatus.
It's tall, its top
reaches beyond the frame.
A small black shape
moves across the sand,
becomes slowly larger,
then vanishes.
The apparatus is put to use again,
though we cannot see the execution.

6 Minutes (Care)

It's a nice day.
Anyone might say so.
The wall is white,
and the sidewalk goes up to the right
at an angle.
The archway is dark.
A couple of steps suggest
there are more.
The dark changes shade
once, and then again.
We hear a step,
then another, and another.
Just enough to make us notice
the two white shoes
on the topmost visible step.
They are perfectly aligned, perfectly still.
And they shine, they are so clean.
Small shoes, for small feet.
One of the shoes moves down a step.
For a minute, nothing, then the foot left behind
shakes, wobbles, and drops down as well.
We see black socks.
We see that the shoes have buckles.
These do not shine.
No, they gleam, they glimmer, they glint, they pop,
    they glow.

All in all, though, they're not that bright.
We see white smooth skin.
And then the feet once again step down.
The whole figure now comes into view.
He is so young.
Such wavy, curly dark hair.
Such little cheeks.
Such little eyes.
To make matters worse,
he is wearing a sailor suit.
Dark blue,
white stripes from shoulder to armpit.
To make matters even worse,
he is smiling.
He turns away from us,
raises one hand
as if beckoning,
says something we cannot hear.
And then he moves forward,
legs straight, robotically,
down the path.
For three steps,
and then one step,
and then he tumbles.
I would expect a cry, but none comes.
He lies flat, as if
something in the sky interested him.
There is a siren,
probably on the next block.

And then comes a dog,
or something like it.
It is grayish-white.
It has a long snout,
long tail.
It is walking slowly.
The boy happens to have fallen near a light post.
The animal stops at the post, sniffs it.
Then its mouth opens, stays open.
For several seconds.
When the sun hits its eyes,
they appear hollow
even as they glimmer.
The boy has rolled over at this point
and is watching the animal.
He has no expression on his face.
His lips are pursed.
The animal does not notice the boy,
shaking its head vigorously, exiting
at the same pace at which it entered.
The boy sits up,
looks at the camera briefly,
and then begins to cry.
Pretty loudly, too—the sound pierces,
even with this poor sound quality.
A woman in a white sundress
and white tank top
bursts out of the archway.

She runs to the boy, kneels next to him.
Her words are almost incomprehensible,
but we do pick up the word "not,"
as we might expect.
The woman leads the boy
back through the archway.
His head is bowed.
The dark changes shade.
There is a click.
A car alarm goes off, and stays off.

7 Minutes

The baby's head
fills most of the screen,
leaving some hot pink spots
in the corners.
The baby smiles,
shows what there are of its teeth
as a title flashes,
Japanese characters,
English yellow subtitles:
Crazed baby what?
The music in the background could be
called rinky-dink, awkwardly playful,
making too much of an effort to be happy,
or perhaps simply bad.
The baby looks right at us,
rocks its head back and forth,
then reaches its swollen right hand up
to grab at its head and,
miraculously producing a zipper from nowhere,
unzips it just above the eyebrows.
The baby then pulls the head open with its left hand,
half the skull flopping open with a creak.
Using both hands, the baby withdraws a pear,
a stone, a simple hammer, an arrow, a tricycle wheel,
a pencil, a toy bead necklace, a shoe, a toy horse, a
     wagon,

a small train, a model car, a toy airplane, a toy GI, a
    toy Indian,
a small red camera, a small megaphone, a miniature
    Victrola, a vinyl record,
a pair of socks, a pair of shoes, a wallet, a comb, a tiny
    flask, a knife, a credit card,
all of these flipped into the pink air
with a hoot of a slide whistle,
one flip before vanishing.
When the task is complete,
the baby closes itself up
and lies down, arms flat, filling the width of the screen.
Then with a yell that could be called a yawp,
the baby flips
onto its feet,
defining an s-curve as it rises.
It raises both arms,
and a
!!
appears above him.
A door opens behind him,
or at least the sound of a door can be heard.
The baby looks around
and at this point
the film breaks
and the lights come up, and we realize
we may have stopped breathing
for a moment or two.

8 Minutes (Rain)

Off a long highway
in Nebraska
there is a one-story building
covered, all the way around,
with yellow panels.
A door, roughly in the center
of the front of the house.
Two windows, four panes each,
one on either side of the door.
We cannot see the back of the house,
nor either of its sides.
We can, however, tell
that behind the house lies a tall, large, round, plastic
    beaker
with striations up its sides
that must, at closer look, be numbers
meant to indicate a volume filled.
The house sits in a clearing.
Beyond the beaker
is a field of tall grains, probably wheat.
The wheat is cordoned off
with a three-foot high wire fence.
There is a little circular driveway in front of the house,
paved with gravel,
empty.
There is a rumbling that continues

for several minutes,
first softer, then louder, soon
right on top of us.
A mid-sized Datsun, maroon, pulls up in front of
    the building.
A man emerges.
He is wearing black faded jeans,
a blue faded shirt,
pointed shoes we'd suspect are boots.
He goes into the house.
Nothing.
A hawk flies into the frame, lands on the roof.
Nothing.
Then the man leaves the house with a clipboard
    under an arm,
walks back to the marked tube.
He stands beside it, bends down, puts one hand to
    his forehead
to block the sun.
He straightens, writes something on the clipboard,
walks back around to the front of the house
before re-entering it.
He does not emerge again.
It rains.
Rains for the next few days, in fact,
though we see but a fraction of the rainfall
here, in the auditorium.
The film ends too soon to reveal anything else.

10 Minutes

We see a broad valley,
sloping on both sides.
The valley is not overgrown.
Every eight to ten feet,
there is a green shrub.
The shrubs are roughly two feet tall,
though sometimes shorter.
There is a sound that lasts for eleven seconds,
a hand grazing a microphone.
There are two voices talking,
both young and female.
The light is good
because the sky is blue.
From the left comes a tiny gray shape,
falling from the top corner
very, very slowly,
down, down, finally leveling out,
leaving a white trail behind it.
The gray shape grows as it moves,
suggesting approach.
The voices' pitch has gotten higher,
slightly, though they laugh on occasion.
Finally it is evident that something has fallen
from the plane, or was dropped.
A pink finger appears on the right-hand side,
    pointing up.

The little dot grows a parachute,
and its descent slows.
Touching down is rough;
the human figure staggers as it reaches Earth.
The voices wince together as it happens.
Then nothing,
then we become aware
that the figure is walking towards us.
It is all in white, walking fairly vigorously.
The voices are talking, but the wind and the noise
make it hard for us to hear them.
They aren't necessarily saying anything with
    compassion,
or at least the volume and the intensity of the speech
do not suggest that.
The figure, as it gets closer, reveals itself
to be an older man, wearing a white suit,
white shirt, white pants, white socks, white shoes,
walking energetically, pumping the left arm
vigorously, almost swinging it in a circle,
possibly to maintain balance,
possibly to accrue emphasis.
The voices stop, and it becomes evident
that someone knows the new arrival,
one of the voices knows him.
It's difficult to trace the reasons for this conclusion;
it could just be a matter of pitch.
In any case, he takes the camera when he draws near
    enough.

We only catch a brief glimpse of him, enough
to tell he shaves each day, that he is in his mid-seventies,
that he likes to maintain an affect of happiness,
that he may well be happy, that
he wants the camera, because there is something he
    wants to film,
and that something is
grass. And sky. And hills of grass.
And clouds that disrupt. And clouds that have
    dissipated.
No people. No faces. No room left for other humans
at this small and inscrutable
point.

12 Minutes (Patience)

The height of the buildings
suggests the Midwest,
along with the bleak combination
of phone wires, water towers, and grain silos,
though we can't know the setting.
The train moves too quickly.
A girl sits beside the window.
She watches the landscape the train leaves.
Sharp features, dark eyebrows, pale lips,
head scarf, tank top, hands limp in lap.
On the seat between us and her,
a large canvas bag.
Protruding from the bag,
a book's corner, a bottle's top,
and a box, probably for expensive clothing.
The girl expresses nothing.
She bites a fingernail, yanks her hand away,
turns to go through her bag.
Freeze.
Black block letters appear on the screen:

WHERE IS THE GHOST
then
IN THIS PICTURE
then

?

She takes a bag of seeds from the bag,
probably sunflower seeds.
She eats them, spits the husks
on the floor in front of her.
She looks around, almost at us, quickly.
No one sees, right?
She crumples the bag, wads it up,
throws it on the floor, tucks it under her seat,
two quick kicks.
One small finger goes to the window,
draws downward,
then over,
then back up,
then back
to its origin point.
In the square's center
she draws a tree-like shape
one suspects is much like
the trees outside.
The train slows.
She looks around,
stops drawing on the window,
settles herself,
waiting.
And one or two seconds later,
a man in a blue track suit

with a white stripe down its side
sits beside her
after placing a large black duffel
containing two or three cumbersome objects
not meant to be placed in a duffel
in the overhead rack,
after a few tries.
For one minute and a few seconds,
they ride along quietly.
Both sway
as the train sways.
Then the man folds his arms.
Though the track suit blurs their shape,
the angle of his arms when crossed
suggests a lot of muscles.
Twenty seconds of silence
in which the girl sits with her eyes closed, not
    sleeping,
and the man stares straight forward.
Licking his lips occasionally,
he uncrosses his arms.
In so doing, he jostles the girl.
She twists to look at him, then
returns to her earlier state,
staring straight ahead.
He twists, as well,
in almost the same manner.

They do not look at each other.
He crosses his arms, again jostling her.
Again a twist, another twist.
She opens her mouth, closes it.
He turns, looks at her
for seven to nine seconds,
we can't be sure.
She looks back, jerks her head back
in exasperation.
He does the same.
A man walks past them.
He, too, wears a blue track suit.
They talk to each other
in a language we don't know,
occasionally looking at the girl.
The screen freezes.
In red capitals:

WE ARE HAUNTED

then

YOU KNOW

then

IT'S TRUE.

The picture blurs, and blurs more.
We see nothing.

16 Minutes

These hills are of indeterminate origin.
Three men stand beside one of them.
We come closer to the men,
and we find that they,
too,
cannot be fully identified,
faces brown,
granular the best way to say it,
is it dust or just the way of skin,
not sure with the fusky lens.
From the way they swivel,
it is clear they are talking,
to each other we assume,
though not taking their attention off their task,
which at the moment involves facing one direction
    intensely,
all the while holding rifles,
all three of them,
the same rifles,
elaborate contraptions,
almost foolish-looking,
but the dusk gives them a timeless vagueness.
The minutes move,
this is all we can say,
and the men move less.

After four minutes,
stand,
swivel,
stand,
a sandstorm starts,
stops.
They all twitch the same way,
at the same moment,
disgruntled.
One of them walks a few steps,
turns around quickly,
almost prissily,
walks back to his original spot.
After three more minutes with these men,
we still do not understand,
probably.
Their clothing is very similar,
it looks brown or burnt red,
and they fill their clothes in varying degrees.
The beefy one,
those pants and that shirt,
could they burst?
The other two,
they're skinny,
their clothes will always be too big,
and yet here they're bigger.
They all turn together again.

What,
another burst of sand?
No,
a sound.
Which is not to say there has been no sound yet,
though it has been the same sound,
of wind,
and of a flapping,
no referent to it on the screen.
They are still for just over a minute,
then they raise their rifles.
They all point in the same direction,
stay like that,
like that,
until one of them fires.
The wind has blown so loudly that we do not hear
    the shot,
only see a pop of orange fire at the tip of one
    contraption,
see it jump slightly.
One of the men,
standing some ways from the others,
fires twice,
then lowers his gun.
The others,
after an interval,
lower their guns too.

One of them,
the one who hasn't fired yet,
turns around.
The one standing next to him,
the beefy one,
turns around.
Then the other.
They face this way for a number of minutes.
Then,
just out of sync,
they turn once more.
An explosion occurs.
We cannot see them.
When the smoke is gone,
they are gone too.

Acknowledgments

Grateful acknowledgment is made to editors of the journals in which the following poems first appeared, in slightly different form and with different titles:

New American Writing: "7 by 24"

Columbia: A Journal of Literature and Art: "4 by 4," "10 by 12"

Tarpaulin Sky: "10 Minutes"

Free Verse: "5 by 5"

No Tell Motel: "5 by 7," "9 by 9," "19 by 19," "3 Minutes (The Ant)"

About the Author

Winner of the Fifth Annual *Boston Review* Poetry Contest, Max Winter's poems appear in *Free Verse, New American Writing, Ploughshares, The Paris Review, Colorado Review, Volt, The Yale Review, The Canary, Denver Quarterly, First Intensity, GutCult, TYPO,* and *New Young American Poets* (Southern Illinois, 2000). He has published reviews in *The New York Times, The Washington Post, The San Francisco Chronicle, Newsday,* and *BOMB.* He is a Poetry Editor of *Fence.*

TARPAULIN SKY PRESS
CURRENT & FORTHCOMING TITLES

[one love affair]*, by Jenny Boully
Perfectbound & handbound editions

Body Language, by Mark Cunningham
Perfectbound & handbound editions

Attempts at a Life, by Danielle Dutton
Perfectbound & handbound editions

32 Pedals and 47 Stops, by Sandy Florian
Chapbook

Figures for a Darkroom Voice, by Noah Eli Gordon
and Joshua Marie Wilkinson
Perfectbound & handbound editions

Nylund, the Sarcographer, by Joyelle McSweeney
Perfectbound & handbound editions

Give Up, by Andrew Michael Roberts
Chapbook

A Mirror to Shatter the Hammer, by Chad Sweeney
Chapbook

www.tarpaulinsky.com